would develop fully and automatically in a secure and happy home, *but this is not necessarily so.* Restricted space, or surroundings too restrained by adult standards of orderliness, can also 'tidy up' out of ex̶_____ ̶t̶h̶i̶s̶ priceless potential of intelligence ar̶_____ her dull and already in̶_____

The first tw̶_____ ̶i̶i̶rd year is one of expa...̶_̶_̶_̶ activity. The fourth year sees the development of a more sociable attitude, a greater expansion of imaginative play and a more agreeable attitude towards other children.

Maybe there are plenty of toys in the home, but do these contribute to your child's development? His toys should be those which are sturdy, simple and adaptable and which encourage both imagination and dexterity. Complexity is a definite obstruction to imagination. This is why kitchen junk – cartons, plastic bottles, etc. – is so useful.

Cartons and bottles will stack and build like bricks; plastic bottles can be cut or shaped for water or sand play or as fitting toys – all giving good opportunities for helping your child's development, once you realise the significance of these materials to him. *The subsequent purchase of a really worth-while toy is then the more easily afforded.*

By the age of three, your child may have an established interest in picture and story books which have been read to him and talked about with him. In most public libraries there is a section for the under-fives, with a wide variety of colourful picture books and story books for reading aloud.

Your child's vocabulary, so vital to mental and emotional development, will be growing rapidly during his third and fourth year. However, this will depend largely on the attitude of grown-ups – who should always be ready to talk with a child on all topics likely to interest, educate or amuse. This book is intended to help and stimulate all parents who realise the importance of using to the full those situations and materials most likely to help develop their child's potential for learning.

BOOK 3
Three to four years

THE LADYBIRD 'UNDER FIVE' SERIES

Learning
with
Mother

by ETHEL and HARRY WINGFIELD

Publishers: Ladybird Books Ltd . Loughborough
© Ladybird Books Ltd (formerly Wills & Hepworth Ltd) 1970
Printed in England

Sand   At four years of age, sand is still experimental and essential play material; essential because it is material into which a child can project his or her own ideas. Pieces of cardboard make good bridges, cartons can become houses and garages, plastic containers serve as petrol pumps and, minus ends, become tunnels, etc. Twigs can be used as trees, sticks in cotton reels as road signs. Model cars and farmyard animals can all be used in this development of sand play.

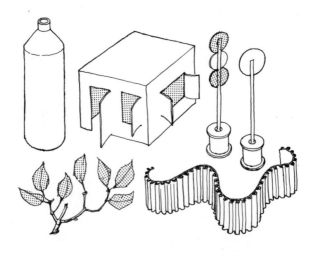

Discuss the picture with your child – and be a good listener. Help your child to name the objects which the children have made and are using, such as bridges, fences, road signs, etc.

4

0 7214 0266 6

bus
stop

Visiting a place of interest

Is there any place which you could visit to look at boats? Many large cities have canal basins, for instance. Your child could make a scrap-book about boats cut from magazines and newspapers. However roughly they are cut out by the child, he will be gaining in knowledge and manual skill by his efforts.

You could print the word 'Boats' on the cover, as well as his own name. To the child, printed words are symbols which in time he will come to recognise and associate with objects and people. However, it is wiser to avoid any deliberate attempt to teach him to read at this age.

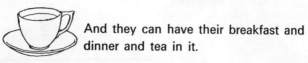

This is a boat that people live in.

They sleep in it.

They cook in it.

They clean their teeth in it.

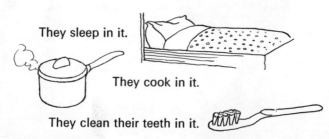

And they can have their breakfast and dinner and tea in it.

Discuss the pictures with your child.

Plastic boats   Something for Father to make!
Here are boats cut from plastic
containers, each with its own little man. Probably the only
contribution the child will be capable of making to this
piece of hand-work is to slot the little men into position,
but by watching objects being made from junk material,
his own ideas and imagination are encouraged.

Then let your child discover and create for himself,
improvising with any safe junk material.

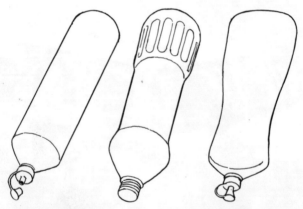

Discuss the picture with your child. Encourage
your child to say which boats are long, and which one is
round. Let your child show you with hand actions what
is meant by long and what is meant by round. Ask what
other differences he can see. He may need some prompting
from you, and you could bring in the word 'different',
'sail' and 'mast'. You could also say the nursery
rhyme: "Rub a dub dub." **Always be a good listener
to anything he or she has to say.**

Another interesting outing

Most children enjoy a visit to the Zoo, and by the age of three years have handled toy animals and looked at animal picture books. Their interest may lie where you least expect – in the aquarium or aviary, for instance. Children love to try out the tongue-twisting names of some of the creatures such as cockatoo, chimpanzee, marmoset, hippopotamus, etc. Back home, keep up this interest with pictures and conversation, and perhaps another scrap-book.

Make up some rhymes together – it is easier than you may think! Humour has great appeal for children, who love to laugh at the ridiculous. Humour can be helpful and, by its use, facts and knowledge are made acceptable to the small child.

Discuss the picture with your child. You can say what big teeth the Hippopotamus has, and how large he is and what thick, tough skin he has. Feel how smooth your own skin is.

Ask your child if he can think of other animals that have rough or smooth skin, or feathers, hair or fur.

Pretence play   Children play out real life experiences in pretence play. For instance, after a visit to the Zoo they will pretend to be the animals they have seen, or they will pretend to be keepers and talk about feeding fish to the penguins, meat to the lions or hay to the zebras.

The more knowledge they acquire during these outings, particularly if there is plenty of conversation accompanying them, the more involved, interesting and educational their pretence play becomes for them. This is the natural way in which words and information become permanently fixed in a child's mind.

Parents can do much to help by allowing a collection of junk material to be at hand. Even Mummy is sometimes necessary. "Mummy, be a giraffe, just for a minute, please!"

Penguin

Tiger

You can make the 'penguin' from a large paper bag, with the flippers cut to fit over the arms and held to the wrists with string or sellotape. The 'tiger' is a paper smock, the halves pinned together and painted. The tiger's ears are of thin card on string or elastic. The 'snake' is four stockings sewn together and stuffed with torn newspaper.

Discuss the picture with your child. Explain that the children are pretending to be animals at feeding time. Read the notices together and point out which animals are which. **Be a good listener to anything your child might wish to say.**

monkey
and
snake

ZOO

penguin

fish

pay
here

tiger

Visiting the dentist

Here is a picture which is intended to encourage your child to ask questions. If you think carefully about your answers, you can dispel many of the fears that unusual situations — such as a visit to the dentist — may arouse. For instance, you can explain that the odd-looking chair tilts back to help the dentist see inside your mouth more easily, that the small mirror on a handle is used to see the back of the teeth. You can explain that if we go to see him often, the dentist will help to take care of our teeth, but we must also do this ourselves by brushing them after meals. Say that the little boy in the picture had taken care of his teeth, and the dentist did not have to do anything at all to them.

Explain also that some foods help to clean our teeth: foods such as pieces of apple, carrot and celery. Some foods, such as sweets and sweet drinks, are bad for our teeth if we have too many each day.

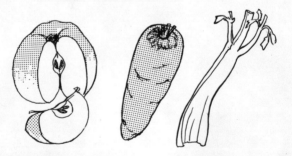

Discuss the picture with your child. Have fun referring back to the huge teeth of the hippopotamus and compare them with your own.

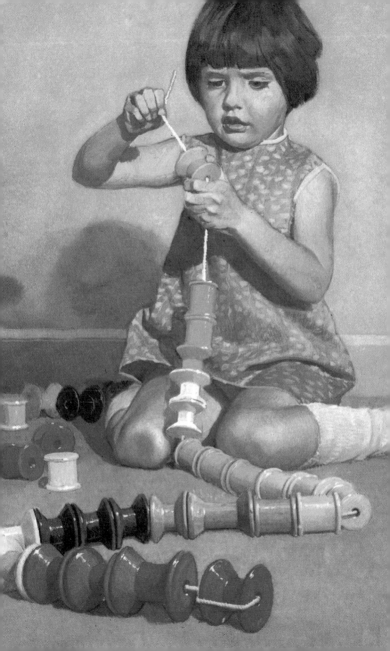

Enjoyable water play

Blowing bubbles is an enjoyable way of playing with water. Bubble pipes are not really necessary; plastic tubing works just as well. Washing-up liquid can be added to the water. You may have to make sure that your child blows and does not suck, so it would be wise for him (or her) first to practise blowing in water without any washing-up liquid in it.

If a wire ring is used for blowing bubbles, this can be dipped in washing-up liquid which has not been diluted with water.

Discuss the picture. Ask your child to point to the largest bubbles and the smallest. Show him how round the bubbles are – and how they sparkle. **Be a good listener to anything your child says about the picture.**

The convalescent child

Most children are ill at some time during their pre-school years. When they are getting better, you can help the time to pass happily and usefully by providing some tray toys and occupations. Some of these can be bought; for example: snap cards, 'Happy Families' and picture dominoes. With all these games, the minimum of demonstration will enable a child to play happily alone, matching up the cards or playing out the picture dominoes in the usual way.

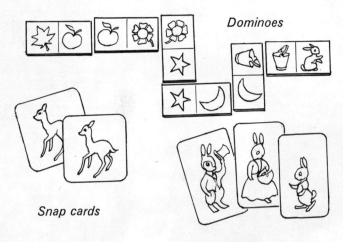

Dominoes

Snap cards

Animal Families

Talk about the picture — Say that the little girl's grandfather is playing a game with her, that he wears spectacles and that she is telling him what to do. **Be a good listener to anything your child wishes to say.**

The convalescent child

Pipe cleaner figures are great fun, but they contain wire which can scratch, so a little care is needed when handling. More intricate models can be made by adults to entertain a child if pieces of material, beads, wool or paper are sellotaped on. These will amuse your child and will be an encouragement to his or her own later imaginative efforts.

Talk about the picture. Ask your child to tell you what figures the grandmother and her grand-daughter have made, and whether there are any numbers among them. **Be a good listener.**

The convalescent child

Using a paper bag of a suitable size, cut eyes, nose and mouth. Give the corners a twist for ears. Stuff with toilet paper and insert hand and fingers (securing at wrist with a rubber band), or tie onto an empty toilet roll. What have we made? Perhaps the big, bad Wolf! Father Bear! or a clown! They may well be all your ideas or perhaps your child's, but he or she will be just as enchanted with them. You could give names to the puppets.

Start your child off on this pretence play and you may be surprised at the imaginative response. Fun and laughter together are a wonderful tonic for a child.

Talk about the picture. Ask what your child thinks the puppet heads look like. Make a puppet head together. Be sure never to use a plastic bag, and never to leave one near a child. **Be a good listener.**

The convalescent child

An action rhyme which will amuse a sick child. Touch each toe in turn as you say each line, starting with the big toe.

This little pig went to market,

This little pig stayed at home;

This little pig had roast beef.

This little pig had none;

And this little pig cried "wee wee wee" all the way home.

Discuss the picture with your child.

48

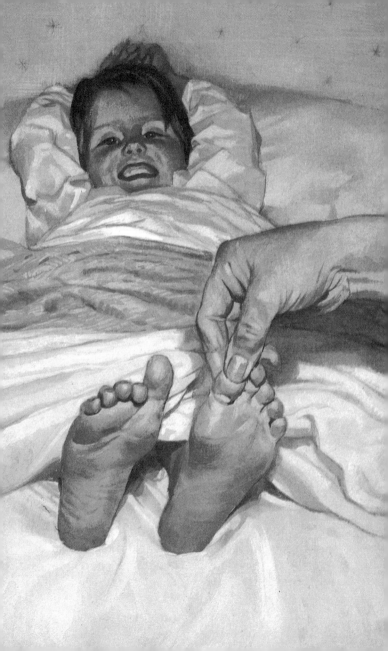

The convalescent child

Old mail-order catalogues give children a lot of pleasure in a variety of ways. They love to recognise and choose from the shoes, toys, handbags, clothes and household articles illustrated.

A wonderful amount of cutting practice can be had in this way. Attempts which are poor at first improve rapidly with so large an amount of material available. Cutting is made easier if you tear out the whole page first, as the catalogues are too cumbersome for a child to handle.

Discuss the picture with your child. Ask what the little girl is cutting out, what she is holding, and what are some of the pictures in the catalogue. **Be a good listener to any comments.**

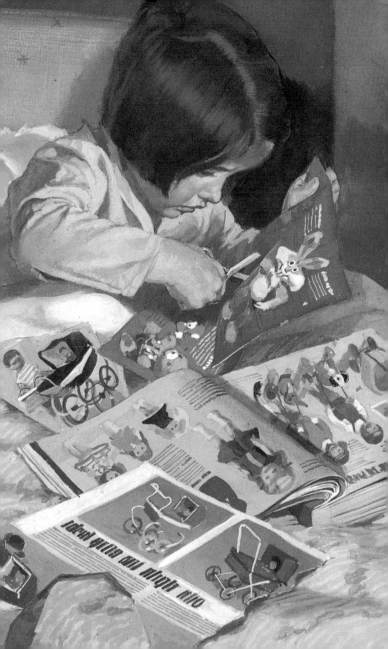

Ask your child to find the page from which each picture is taken, and talk about what is happening there.

A home-made xylophone

Here is a home-made xylophone that will provide another kind of noise experience.

Pour water into bottles in varying amounts. Those bottles with more water play lower notes than those with less water, and by adjusting the amount of water in each bottle, and lightly touching them with a pencil or spoon, you will be able to play simple tunes, such as ''Three Blind Mice'' or ''Ding Dong Bell''.

By running a pencil along from the first to the last bottle, a child can play all the notes of an octave. This will sound like a peal of bells, and seem as clever to him as the tunes you can play.

Discuss the picture with your child.

Familiar people   Children should be encouraged to watch out for familiar people at their everyday work — the dustman, the milk-man, the baker, the bus driver and the postman.

You can talk about what these people do. You can say, for instance, that unless the bus driver gets up early in the morning, has his breakfast and gets to the bus garage early, people who work in shops, offices and factories, and children who go to school on the bus, would not be able to arrive in time.

Tell your child about letters being sorted in special mail trains which run all through the night while he is asleep. Encourage questions, and if you yourself do not know all the answers, find out the facts together from the many informative Ladybird books.

Discuss the picture with your child and be a good listener.

More about the importance of pretence play

A child who sees the postman empty a letter-box is likely to want to do this himself by playing the postman collecting and delivering letters. A large carton adapted by mother (the one illustrated was a banana box), topped by a round tray – plus a few old cards or envelopes – are all that is needed. Try making available as much junk material as possible and leaving your child to select what he needs for such games.

This type of pretence play is very essential to normal development. It fixes knowledge and experience into a child's mind. One could say that it helps to digest information.

Pretence play does not always need to be constructive; even destructive play has its value. For example, your child could get great satisfaction from pretending that his letter-box has been crashed into or knocked over. You may find him sitting on a flattened box among scattered cards, talking to himself about 'crashing', 'banging', 'knocking-over' – and so on. Do not worry about this – the box can easily be stood up again. Being destructive in such cases need represent no more than a healthy curiosity or desire to experiment, and junk material, being expendable, is ideal for the purpose. With such material at his disposal, he is far less likely to want to damage his books and toys.

Discuss the picture with your child and be a good listener.

Home-made toy

Cotton-reels, painted with household paint in a variety of colours (lead-free paint, of course), make a very good toy. In threading them a child is developing hand and eye co-ordination and manipulative skill, as well as distinguishing between colours. This toy can also be used for counting practice.

Use ordinary string for threading, knotting it at one end and with the threading-end stiffened with glue for about three inches. This ample length of stiffened string makes first attempts at threading less disappointing than limp string, which might fail to go through the hole and appear, as hoped, at the other end.

Discuss the picture. Ask your child to name the colours and count the number of reels in each colour.

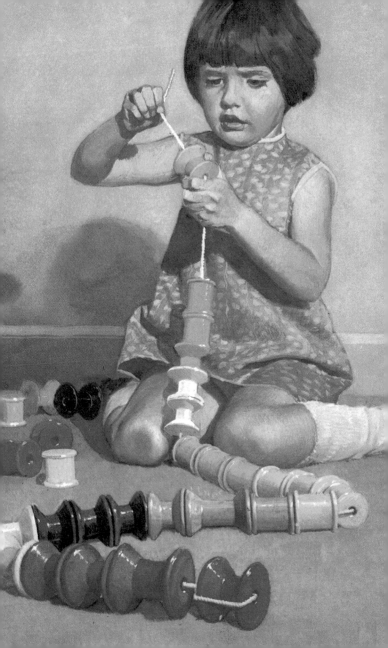

Enjoyable water play

Blowing bubbles is an enjoyable way of playing with water. Bubble pipes are not really necessary; plastic tubing works just as well. Washing-up liquid can be added to the water. You may have to make sure that your child blows and does not suck, so it would be wise for him (or her) first to practise blowing in water without any washing-up liquid in it.

If a wire ring is used for blowing bubbles, this can be dipped in washing-up liquid which has not been diluted with water.

Discuss the picture. Ask your child to point to the largest bubbles and the smallest. Show him how round the bubbles are – and how they sparkle. **Be a good listener to anything your child says about the picture.**

The convalescent child

Most children are ill at some time during their pre-school years. When they are getting better, you can help the time to pass happily and usefully by providing some tray toys and occupations. Some of these can be bought; for example: snap cards, 'Happy Families' and picture dominoes. With all these games, the minimum of demonstration will enable a child to play happily alone, matching up the cards or playing out the picture dominoes in the usual way.

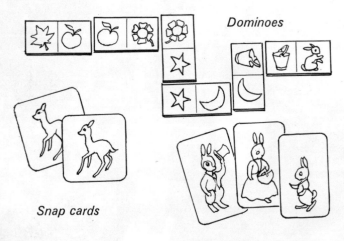

Dominoes

Snap cards

Animal Families

Talk about the picture — Say that the little girl's grandfather is playing a game with her, that he wears spectacles and that she is telling him what to do. **Be a good listener to anything your child wishes to say.**

The convalescent child

Pipe cleaner figures are great fun, but they contain wire which can scratch, so a little care is needed when handling. More intricate models can be made by adults to entertain a child if pieces of material, beads, wool or paper are sellotaped on. These will amuse your child and will be an encouragement to his or her own later imaginative efforts.

Talk about the picture. Ask your child to tell you what figures the grandmother and her grand-daughter have made, and whether there are any numbers among them. **Be a good listener.**

The convalescent child

Using a paper bag of a suitable size, cut eyes, nose and mouth. Give the corners a twist for ears. Stuff with toilet paper and insert hand and fingers (securing at wrist with a rubber band), or tie onto an empty toilet roll. What have we made? Perhaps the big, bad Wolf! Father Bear! or a clown! They may well be all your ideas or perhaps your child's, but he or she will be just as enchanted with them. You could give names to the puppets.

Start your child off on this pretence play and you may be surprised at the imaginative response. Fun and laughter together are a wonderful tonic for a child.

Talk about the picture. Ask what your child thinks the puppet heads look like. Make a puppet head together. Be sure never to use a plastic bag, and never to leave one near a child. **Be a good listener.**

The convalescent child

An action rhyme which will amuse a sick child. Touch each toe in turn as you say each line, starting with the big toe.

This little pig went to market,

This little pig stayed at home;

This little pig had roast beef.

This little pig had none;

And this little pig cried "wee wee wee" all the way home.

Discuss the picture with your child.

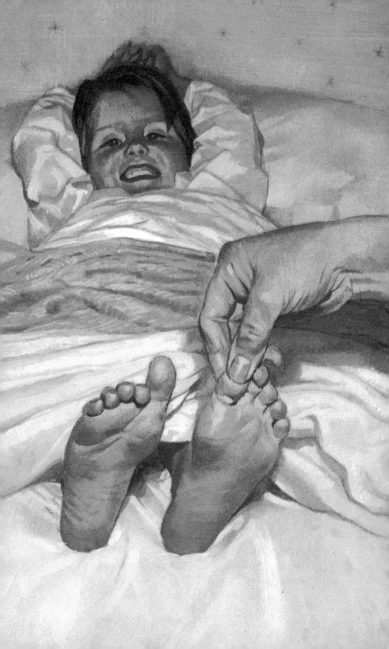

The convalescent child

Old mail-order catalogues give children a lot of pleasure in a variety of ways. They love to recognise and choose from the shoes, toys, handbags, clothes and household articles illustrated.

A wonderful amount of cutting practice can be had in this way. Attempts which are poor at first improve rapidly with so large an amount of material available. Cutting is made easier if you tear out the whole page first, as the catalogues are too cumbersome for a child to handle.

Discuss the picture with your child. Ask what the little girl is cutting out, what she is holding, and what are some of the pictures in the catalogue. **Be a good listener to any comments.**

Ask your child to find the page from which each picture is taken, and talk about what is happening there.